A WART SNAKE
IN A FIG TREE

THE DIAL PRESS
NEW YORK

WORDS BY
GEORGE MENDOZA

PICTURES BY
ETIENNE DELESSERT

A WART SNAKE
N A FIG TREE

Text copyright © 1968 by George Mendoza. Pictures copyright © 1968 by Etienne Delessert.
All rights reserved. Library of Congress catalog card number: 68-28733. Printed in the
United States of America. First Pied Piper Printing. A WART SNAKE IN A FIG TREE
is published in a hardcover edition by The Dial Press, 1 Dag Hammarskjold Plaza, New
York, New York 10017. ISBN 0-8037-9446-0

For Eleonore and Etienne

On the first day of Christmas my true love gave to me a wart snake in a fig tree.

On the second day of Christmas my true love gave to me two bags of soot and a wart snake in a fig tree.

On the third day of Christmas my true love gave to me three cobwebs, two bags of soot, and a wart snake in a fig tree.

On the fourth day of Christmas my true love gave to me four raven wings, three cobwebs, two bags of soot, and a wart snake in a fig tree.

On the fifth day of Christmas my true love gave to me five useless things, four raven wings, three cobwebs, two bags of soot, and a wart snake in a fig tree.

On the sixth day of Christmas my true love gave to me six shadows lurking, five useless things, four raven wings, three cobwebs, two bags of soot, and a wart snake in a fig tree.

On the seventh day of Christmas my true love gave to me seven ghouls acaroling, six shadows lurking, five useless things, four raven wings, three cobwebs, two bags of soot, and a wart snake in a fig tree.

On the eighth day of Christmas my true love gave to me eight snow wolves wailing, seven ghouls acaroling, six shadows lurking, five useless things, four raven wings, three cobwebs, two bags of soot, and a wart snake in a fig tree.

On the ninth day of Christmas my true love gave to me nine nightmares galloping, eight snow wolves wailing, seven ghouls acaroling, six shadows lurking, five useless things, four raven wings, three cobwebs, two bags of soot, and a wart snake in a fig tree.

On the tenth day of Christmas my true love gave to me ten devils grinning, nine nightmares galloping, eight snow wolves wailing, seven ghouls acaroling, six shadows lurking, five useless things, four raven wings, three cobwebs, two bags of soot, and a wart snake in a fig tree.

On the eleventh day of Christmas my true love gave to me eleven lizards boiling, ten devils grinning, nine nightmares galloping, eight snow wolves wailing, seven ghouls acaroling, six shadows lurking, five useless things, four raven wings, three cobwebs, two bags of soot, and a wart snake in a fig tree.

On the twelfth day of Christmas my true love gave to me twelve days of raining, eleven lizards boiling, ten devils grinning, nine nightmares galloping, eight snow wolves wailing, seven ghouls acaroling, six shadows lurking, five useless things, four raven wings, three cobwebs, two bags of soot, and a wart snake in a fig tree.

Gaily

1. On the first day of Christ - mas my true love gave to me A wart snake in a fig tree.__ 2. On the se - cond day of Christ - mas my true love gave to me two bags of soot and a wart snake in a fig tree. 3. On the third day of Christ - mas my true love gave to me three cob - webs, two bags of soot, and a wart snake in a fig tree.__ 4. On the fourth day of Christ - mas my true love gave to me four ra - ven wings, three cob - webs, two bags of soot, and a wart snake in a fig

tree.___ 5. On the fifth day of Christ - mas my true love gave to me
five use - less things, four___ ra - ven wings, three cob - webs,
two___ bags of soot, and a wart snake in a fig tree.___

Repeat for seventh day to twelfth day

6. On the sixth day of Christ - mas my true love gave to me
7. On the seventh day_____ *etc.*

six shad - ows lurk - ing, *(to 5)* five use - less things, four ra - ven wings,
seven ghouls a - carol - ing, *(to 6)*
eight snow wolves wail - ing, *(to 7)*
nine night - mares gallop - ing, *(to 8)*
ten dev - ils grin - ning, *(to 9)*
eleven liz - ards boil - ing, *(to 10)*
twelve days of rain - ing, *(to 11)*

three cob - webs, two___ bags of soot, and a wart snake in a fig tree.___

The End